How to Invest in the Stock Market

Investing in Dividend Stocks for Beginners and How to Read Stock Charts (2 Manuscripts in 1 Book)

By D.K. Livingston

Investing in Dividend Stocks for Beginners

How to Invest for Passive Income (Mutual Funds, ETFs, and Index Funds)

By D.K. Livingston

Text Copyright © 2019 D.K. Livingston

All Rights Reserved

No part of this book may be reproduced

in any way without the written

permission of the author.

Disclaimer:

The views expressed within this book are those of the author alone. The information contained within this book is based on the opinions, experiences, and observations of the author and is provided "AS-IS". No warranties of any kind are made. Neither the author nor publisher are engaged in rendering professional services of any kind. Neither the author nor publisher will assume liability or responsibility for any loss or damage related directly or indirectly to the information contained within this book.

The author has attempted to be as accurate as possible with the information contained within this book. Neither the author nor publisher will assume responsibility or liability for any errors, omissions, inconsistencies, or inaccuracies.

Table of Contents

Introduction 1
How Dividends Work 4
ETFs vs Mutual Funds vs Index Funds 6
How to Research Mutual Funds and ETFs 7
How to Select a Broker that is Right for You 8
How to Reduce Risk 14
How to Build a Portfolio 20
How to Find Companies that are Likely to Raise their Dividends ... 24
How to Select Dividend-Paying Stocks 28
Closing 30
Introduction 35
Technical Analysis vs Fundamental Analysis 39
How to Understand the Different Types of Candlesticks 41
How to Know the Price Range of a Trading Period 41
How to Know Where the Opening and Closing of a Time frame is 43
Candlestick Names and Definitions 44
How to Use Candlesticks to Avoid Losses 45
Candlestick Patterns 49
How to Know if the Share Price is Likely to Ascend or Descend ... 53
How to Use a Chart to See if a Trend is Likely to Reverse 56
How to Identify Buy and Sell Signals on a Chart 60
How to Determine How Far a Share Price May Ascend or Decline 62
Closing 65

Introduction

Whether an investor is interested in individual stocks or diversified index funds, investing in dividend-paying stocks can be a great way to generate passive income.

While share prices rise and fall, a dividend is guaranteed money that can't be taken away from you.

But knowing which dividend-paying stocks to invest in is crucial. Not all passive income opportunities in the financial markets have the same potential for a return on investment.

Although profits from the dividends can be taken right away and used for other things, reinvesting them in other dividend-paying stocks can improve an investor's portfolio more drastically in the long-term.

In other words, sometimes doing less brings better results.

Many full-time traders and investors often take partial profits, and then they leave the rest of the profits in their investment. This allows the investors to reduce some of the risk, while still staying in the game.

But oftentimes, leaving the investment alone can produce more profits than constantly shifting money around in and out of trades.

Generally, dividends are paid out on a quarterly basis (every three months).

Since dividends are essentially guaranteed income, many people tend to invest in securities that pay dividends, especially during financially uncertain times.

Since many investors tend to move their capital into securities that have the guaranteed income of dividends, that can often cause the price of shares to increase, which of course, can generate even more profits for the traders that plan to eventually sell for capital gains.

When news gets released about a company raising it's dividend payout, this can serve as a catalyst, which can cause many investors to buy shares and move the price up higher.

Dividends can be powerful.

Even if you are working full-time at a high-paying job that you are passionate about, it's still important to know how to have your money work for you.

Unexpected situations can arise, such as:

• Injuries

• Illnesses

• Surgery

• Company cutbacks that lead to a reduction in your salary

• Company cutbacks that lead to the loss of your job

• A devastating turn for the worse in management that make working conditions nearly unbearable

• New coworkers that make things extremely difficult for you

Additionally, learning about dividend investing can be a great way to plan for retirement, because social security benefits might not be quite enough to live off of for as long as a person hopes for.

Aside from research, there is not much more work involved.

Although investing in real estate can often involve hiring carpenters, electricians, and paying for ads to fix up a house and sell it, individual stocks and index funds can feel like much less of a hassle when it comes to generating passive income.

After some research is completed, a BUY button is selected inside a brokerage account, and then the security is purchased.

But how does an investor perform effective research?

How can an investor build and manage a portfolio?

How does an investor know how to reduce risk?

This book is intended to educate you on the fundamentals of investing in dividend-producing investments, focusing primarily on mutual funds, as well as provide you with some insight that can be utilized to become a successful investor.

It will cover:

- **How dividends work**

- **How to research mutual funds and ETFs**

- **How to select a broker that is right for you**

- **How to reduce risk**

- **How to build a portfolio**

- **How to find companies that are likely to raise their dividends**

- **and more**

How Dividends Work

Usually, dividends are paid out on a "per share" basis every quarter, so if a company pays a dollar per share, a person with a hundred shares will generate $100 in dividend income every three months.

It is considered a cash payment that is made possible by the company's earnings, and it's a good way for an investor to make money from a company by investing in it, without having to sell the shares that he or she owns.

A dividend allows the investor to make money from the company without the investor having to give up his or her stake in it.

The only other way to make money from the ownership of a stock without having to sell it is through the use of options strategies.

The managers of a company have to choose what they are going to do with their profits.

They can either choose to reinvest the profits back into their company directly, or they can issue the profits to the investors.

What they decide to do will depend largely on where they stand as a company.

If they feel that share prices will probably not move as high as they did in the past, they might decide to issue "rewards" (dividends) to the shareholders as an incentive to keep them around.

In most cases, when a company is growing at a rapid pace, they won't see much need to offer dividends to shareholders. They might assume that their rapid growth is enough of an incentive to get people to invest in them.

But just because a company offers a dividend, it doesn't necessarily mean that it is no longer growing at a rapid pace.

When a company decides that their days of high-speed growth are behind them, it is likely just a guess.

Personally, I have traded a stock multiple times from a company whose share prices have still been climbing drastically. They offer a dividend, and yet their company seems to be showing no signs of slowing down anytime soon.

The dividend payout is determined by the company's board of directors, who decide how much money gets distributed to the shareholders and how much gets placed back into the company.

Although it seldom happens, sometimes a company will stop issuing dividend payments. It's their right to do so whenever they want.

To give yourself a better chance of not having a company discontinue dividend payments, look for a company that has a long record of issuing them consistently.

Of course, when selecting a dividend-paying company to invest in, it's important to also pay attention to the price performance of the company's shares.

A generous-sounding dividend will not make up for a rapidly declining stock if you plan on selling your shares for profit in the near future.

ETFs vs Mutual Funds vs Index Funds

Since there are so many different things to invest in, it can certainly help to clarify the difference between them.

This chapter will focus on ETFs, mutual funds, and index funds.

ETFs- Exchange-traded funds are bundles of securities that can be traded on an open exchange. Generally, taxation costs and management fees are lower in comparison to those of mutual funds. They can be traded more easily, which allows many investors to view them as more flexible than mutual funds. Pricing information for buys and sells can be obtained in real time. Investors in ETFs are responsible for paying brokerage commissions, management fees, annual fees, as well as other expenses.

Index funds- These funds are not what people invest in directly, as they only act as a mirror for mutual funds. They are a representation of a segment of the market. They can be invested in on an indirect basis through the use of a mutual fund.

Mutual fund- This is a company that gathers money from a large group of investors and invests it in securities. People who invest in mutual funds buy and sell their shares to and from the mutual funds themselves. Investors in mutual funds are responsible for paying sales charges, management fees, annual fees, as well as other expenses. There may also be price uncertainty for an investor of mutual funds because the price at which the investor buys or sells shares might not be calculated until well after the order for the trade has taken place.

If the mutual fund or ETF is based on a 401K or IRA, taxes won't have to be paid until you withdraw money from it.

How to Research Mutual Funds and ETFs

Before investing, you can perform research on a mutual fund of ETF by looking over its prospectus. Reading the prospectus can help you identify the investment strategy and potential risks of the mutual fund or ETF.

The prospectus can be found on the mutual fund's or ETF's website. You can also visit sec.gov/edgar

and download the documents at no charge.

Another option is to call the SEC at their toll-free help line: (800) 732- 0330.

How to Select a Broker that is Right for You

Since different online brokerages have different pros and cons, it's important to choose one that is right for your particular situation.

This chapter will cover some of the most popular online brokers, as well as the pros and cons to each one, how much money they charge per trade via commissions, and what the minimum account balance must be.

Note: Brokers can change their rule structure at anytime, so it's important to visit their websites to verify that the information is current.

E*TRADE

This broker is among the most popular. It was founded in 1982, and their first online trade took place in 1983. They are headquartered in New York City with 30 retail branches across the United States.

Commission fees per trade: $6.95, but only $4.95 with 30 or more trades per quarter

Commission fees for mutual funds: $19.99

Account minimum: $500

Pros

- The platform is known to be beginner-friendly and easy to use

- Offers personalized support and guidance

- Offers independent analyst research

- Has investing tools

- Reduced commission fees for traders who place more than 30 trades per quarter

- Their mobile app makes them more accessible

- Stocks, bonds, options, ETFs, and mutual funds are all available as investment choices

Cons

- There are other brokers that offer smaller commission fees

- There are other brokers that do not require a minimum account balance

Ally

Ally Invest seems to offer a good balance between beginner-friendly and advanced. It's good for beginner investors because there is no minimum account balance required to get started, while the more advanced investor might appreciate their charting, data, and analytical tools.

There are no inactivity fees if the account remains dormant for a while.

Commission fees per trade: $4.95, but only $3.95 with 30 or more trades per quarter

Commission fees for mutual funds: $9.95

Account minimum: $0

Pros

• Lower commission fees than many other brokers

• No minimum account balance requirement

• Customer service is available 24/7

• Tools and informational articles available

• SIPC covered, so up to $250,000 worth of cash funds are protected if *Ally Invest* fails

• Stocks, bonds, options, ETFs, commission-free ETFs, margin accounts, and mutual funds are all available as investment choices

• Offers FOREX trading

• Offers automated portfolio management

Cons

• They do not offer zero-fee transaction for mutual funds

Merrill Edge

Bank of America is their parent company.

Commission fees per trade: $6.95

Account minimum: $0

Pros

• No minimum account balance required

• Customer service available 24/7

• Access to award-winning research

• Has tools that help you make more informed investment decisions

• Stocks, bonds, options, ETFs, mutual funds or professionally managed portfolios are all available as investment choices

• Offers *Market Pro* for active investors

Cons

• There are other brokers that offer cheaper commission fees.

• To qualify for ten $0 online stock and ETF trades per month (the most basic tier), a three-month average balance of at least $20,000 between Bank of America and Merrill Edge accounts must be maintained, which many people might find unrealistic.

AMERITRADE

This brokerage has over 360 branches in the United States.

Commission fees per trade: $6.95

Account minimum: $0

Pros

- No minimum account balance required

- Includes many advanced features

- Investment selection includes equities, options, futures, and FOREX

- Offers personalized coaching via social media, webcasts, and in-person workshops

- Allows the users to "paper trade" for practice without risking real money

- Customer service available 24/7

Cons

- There are other brokers that offer cheaper commission fees.

- Broker-assisted fees are $44.99, which some investors might find expensive.

Fidelity

They used to have an account minimum requirement for mutual funds, but they have now done away with that. They have zero expense ratio for index funds.

Commission fees per trade: $4.95

Account minimum: $0

Pros

- Offers help with planning for retirement and advice on wealth management

- Robust investing tools

- No minimum amount of money required to open an account

- Zero expense ratio index funds

- Zero minimum investment mutual funds

- Customer service available 24/7

- Lower commission fees than many other brokers

- Covered by FDIC and SIPC

Cons

- Need to deposit $50,000-$99,000 to qualify for their promotional offer of 300 free trades over a 2 year period, which some people may find to be too much money.

* * *

If you are feeling indecisive about which online broker to use, know that there is no commitment involved. If you find another broker later on that fits your needs better, you can always switch over.

How to Reduce Risk

Since the financial markets are subject to having ups and downs, it is important to know how to reduce your risk.

One of the best ways to reduce risk as an investor is to diversify.

But it's crucial to know how to diversify.

It makes little sense to buy *Comcast, Sprint, T-Mobile,* and *Verizon,* and then assume that you have diversified your risk correctly.

That's because all of those stocks belong to the same sector.

When building a portfolio, it's important to include stocks from different sectors to diversify the risk factor.

Each industry will have its own set of catalysts.

If the tech industry is declining significantly, an investor can find relief in the fact that his or her portfolio is still doing well because of the investments that were made in the healthcare industry, energy industry, etc.

Oftentimes, when one industry is down, another one will be up. The investors can then cut their losses with the falling stocks, while continuing to invest in the ones that are doing well.

If the losing stocks are sold early enough, the gains from the well-performing stocks can be larger than the losses from the ones that are not performing well.

Here is a list of the different stock sectors, along with some of the big companies that are in them:

Basic Materials

- Ecolab
- International Paper
- Sherwin-Williams
- Valvoline

Consumer Goods

- Ford
- GM
- Home Depot
- Starbucks
- Target
- Wynn

Consumer Staples

- Costco
- Kraft
- Procter and Gamble
- Walmart

Energy

- BP

- Chevron
- Exon
- Kinder Morgan
- Shell

Financial

- Bank of America
- Goldman Sachs
- JPMorgan
- Morgan Stanley
- Nasdaq
- Wells Fargo
- U.S. Bank

Healthcare

- CVS
- Johnson and Johnson
- Merck
- Medtronic
- Pfizer
- United Healthcare

Industrial

- Boeing

- Caterpillar
- Deere
- Delta
- Honeywell
- Lockheed Martin
- Raytheon
- UPS
- 3M

Real Estate

- Aimco
- AvalonBay Communities
- Simon Property Group

Tech

- Adobe
- Apple
- Facebook
- Google
- IBM
- Intel
- Linkedin
- Mastercard

- Microsoft

- Visa

- Yelp

Telecommunications

- AT&T

- Charter

- Comcast

- Disney

- Sprint

- T-Mobile

- Verizon

Utilities

- Duke Energy

- Public Service Enterprise Group

- NextEra

- NRG

- PG&E

- Xcel

* * *

You don't have to invest in every single one of these sectors to become a successful investor, but diversifying can certainly help reduce risk.

Try to invest in at least four different sectors.

How to Build a Portfolio

When it comes to investing in index funds, building a portfolio can be relatively simple. This is because instead of having to pick out over a dozen different individual stocks, the index fund already includes a group of well-balanced stocks in one index.

The diversification is already built in.

Individual stock selection is often better for short-term investing.

Many individual stocks are known for being more volatile than mutual funds and index funds. They might not offer as much stability as an index fund, but when a stock is on an uptrend, the gains can be larger.

When the uptrend of the volatile individual stock looks like it is coming to an end, the stock can be sold for a profit.

That is why individual stocks can be more work to invest in. They must be monitored often, so the investor can identify trend changes that present possible buy and sell signals.

After the stock is sold, the trader must begin the process all over again; researching the market, studying the charts, and planning the next trade.

Index funds are often better for long-term investing, and they generally require less of a "hands on" approach.

There are individual stocks that pay dividends, and there are index funds that pay dividends. But when building a dividend-producing portfolio, it's important to realize which investment strategy matches your risk-profile.

Determining Where You Want Your Money to Go Based on Risk Tolerance, Age, and Financial Goals

When building a portfolio, you need to identify if you want all of your investment money in a mutual fund, or part of it in a mutual fund with the rest of it in individual stocks.

Before you make that decision, it's important to know what type of investor you are.

• Do you see yourself as more of a short-term trader?

• Do you see yourself as more of a long-term investor?

• Do you enjoy taking an active approach to your investments?

• Do you like to "set it and forget it?"

• Do you see trading as sort of an entertaining "video game" that involves money?

• Do you see trading and investing as overly tedious and time consuming?

• Are you willing to lose big in order to win big?

• Are you willing to put a very large amount of money into an investment, just so it can generate a five percent return a year?

• What is your age?

• What will give you peace of mind?

It can take a long time to gain the experience that is necessary to actively trade stocks. If inexperienced investors get impatient and try to actively trade too soon, they will likely lose a large part of their investments. Their money would be better off in a mutual fund.

Typically, the younger the investor is, the more aggressive he or she can be.

A young person losing ten percent of $2,000 isn't as bad as a sixty-year old losing ten percent of $200,000.

Not only is ten percent of $2,000 less significantly less than ten percent of $200,000, but the younger person also has the added advantage of time.

A thirty-year old still has decades to save for retirement. But a sixty-year old might only have several more years to save for retirement, and therefore, less time to make up for the losses.

Looking at Market Capitalization

Market caps are something to take into consideration when you are assessing your risk tolerance.

Small-cap stocks are known to be more volatile the large-cap stocks. This is largely because there is not enough liquidity in small cap stocks to keep them stable. They are often high risk/high reward.

It might only take a million dollars worth of buying or selling power to shift the price of shares for a small-cap stock significantly.

But it would take tens (or hundreds) of millions of dollars to do the same with a large cap stock. Large-cap stocks are typically low risk/low reward.

There are also mid-cap stocks, which could provide a balance for those that are not interested in high risk/high reward or low risk/low reward scenarios.

If you are assessing individual stocks, make sure their market caps match your risk profile.

Calculating the market capitalization is simple:

Number of outstanding shares multiplied by the current market price of one share.

When a mutual fund is categorized by market capitalization, it is referring to the size of the companies that the fund is invested in, not the size of the mutual fund itself.

Small cap- typically less than $2 billion.

Mid-cap- typically $2 billion to $10 billion.

Large cap- typically $10 billion or more.

Dividend Growth Funds

These are diversified funds that allow you to invest in a low-cost ETF. It is essentially a dividend portfolio that has already been put together.

This type of investing is very passive since it is either actively managed by someone else or it simply tracks an index.

Here a some examples of Dividend Growth Funds:

• ishares International Dividend Growth ETF (IGRO)

• ishares Core Dividend Growth ETF (DGRO)

• PowerShares Dividend Achievers Portfolio ETF (PFM)

• PowerShares S&P 500 High Dividend Low Volatility ETF (SPHD)

• SPDR S&P Dividend ETF (SDY)

How to Find Companies that are Likely to Raise their Dividends

Looking at history can help forecast what is likely to happen in the future. When selecting companies to invest in, it can be beneficial to find ones that have a long history of raising their dividend payouts.

If these companies have a long history of raising their dividend, that makes it more likely that they will continue to do so in the future.

Looking over the *S&P Dividend Aristocrats* list will show you companies that have increased their dividends steadily over the years.

S&P Dividend Aristocrats List

- 3M (MMM)
- Abbott Laboratories (ABT)
- AbbVie Inc (ABBV)
- Aflac (AFL)
- Air Products & Chemicals
- A.O. Smith (AOS)
- Archer-Daniels Midland (ADM)
- AT&T (T)

- Automatic Data (ADP)
- Becton Dickinson (BDX)
- Brown-Forman (BF-B)
- Cardinal Health (CAH)
- Caterpillar Inc. (CAT)
- Chevron (CVX)
- Chubb Ltd (CB)
- Cincinnati Fin. (CINF)
- Cintas (CTAS)
- Clorox (CLX)
- Coca-Cola (KO)
- Colgate-Palmolive (CL)
- Consolidated Edison (ED)
- Dover (DOV)
- Emerson Electric (EMR)
- Ecolab (ECL)
- Exxon Mobil (XOM)
- Federal Realty Inv. Trust
- Franklin Resources (BEN)
- General Dynamics (GD)
- Genuine Parts (GPC)

- Hormel Foods (HRL)
- Illinois Tool Works (ITW)
- Johnson & Johnson (JNJ)
- Kimberly-Clark (KMB)
- Leggett & Platt (LEG)
- Linde PLC (LIN)
- Lowe's Companies (LOW)
- McCormick & Co. (MKC)
- McDonald's (MCD)
- Medtronic (MDT)
- Nucor (NUE)
- Pentair (PNR)
- People's United Financial (PBCT)
- PepsiCo (PEP)
- PPG Industries (PPG)
- Procter & Gamble (PG)
- Roper Technologies Inc. (ROP)
- Sherwin-Williams (SHW)
- S&P Global Inc. (SPGI)
- Stanley Black & Decker (SWK)
- Sysco (SYY)

- Target (TGT)

- T.Rowe Price (TROW)

- VF (VFC)

- Walgreens Boots (WBA)

- Wal-Mart Stores (WMT)

- W.W. Grainger (GWW)

If you are looking for an ETF that tracks the *S&P 500 Dividend Aristocrats Index*, look into *The ProShares S&P 500 Dividend Aristocrats ETF* (NOBL).

How to Select Dividend-Paying Stocks

If you go to trading view or another charting platform and look up some of the high-dividend-paying companies, you will probably notice a common pattern among them.

The pattern is that the companies with the highest-paying dividends are usually the ones that have been on a long-term downward trend as far as share prices.

As stated in the introduction chapter, a company may offer a dividend when their growth is slowing down in order to keep investors interested, although that's not always the case.

A high dividend might also mean that not enough money is going back into the company.

When selecting dividend-paying stocks, it's NOT a good idea to simply go after the ones that offer the highest-paying dividends.

Realistically, try to look for a company that offers a 3 to 7 percent dividend payment annually. Companies that offer this percentage are more likely to still be growing.

If you see a company with a very high dividend payout, make sure you check the technical charts to see how they have been doing as a company in the long-term.

If investors only look at the dividends, they might end up paying more money than what the dividends are worth.

For an updated list of dividend stocks, visit: https://www.nasdaq.com/dividend-stocks/

Closing

In many cases, the higher the dividend payout, the lower the return will be as far as price per share when it comes time to sell.

The market is always changing, and it takes a fair amount of research to find a good balance of securities that will maximize profits in the long-term.

Be realistic about your expectations, and don't put all of your investment money into something just for the sake of having it produce dividends.

Non-dividend stocks should not be ignored, as many of them have high potential for good returns.

Dividend stocks should only make up a portion of your entire investment portfolio.

A good way to reduce risk is through diversification, and to diversify effectively, an investor should not limit him/herself to dividend stocks.

Buying low-cost index funds can be a very good way to outperform the investors who are constantly chasing trends.

When selecting dividend stocks, look for companies that are still growing.

Reinvesting the income generated through dividends can certainly add up to good profits over time.

How to Read Stock Charts

Technical Analysis for Beginners, Including Moving Average Trading

By D.K. Livingston

Text Copyright © 2019 D.K. Livingston

All Rights Reserved

No part of this book may be reproduced

in any way without the written

permission of the author.

Disclaimer:

The views expressed within this book are those of the author alone. The information contained within this book is based on the opinions, experiences, and observations of the author and is provided "AS-IS". No warranties of any kind are made. Neither the author nor publisher are engaged in rendering professional services of any kind. Neither the author nor publisher will assume liability or responsibility for any loss or damage related directly or indirectly to the information contained within this book.

The author has attempted to be as accurate as possible with the information contained within this book. Neither the author nor publisher will assume responsibility or liability for any errors, omissions, inconsistencies, or inaccuracies.

Introduction

If you have ever struggled in the financial markets before, you were probably striving to find a solution.

You might have wondered what separates successful traders from unsuccessful ones.

When determining what makes a trader successful, there are a variety of factors that come into play, including:

- **emotional control**

- **risk management**

- **substantial amount of capital**

- **ability to identify intrinsic value of a company or asset**

But even if the above principals are utilized, the investors may still feel like they are going in blind. How does a person know when to buy or sell?

For example, emotional control can prevent a trader from jumping into an investment too soon. But how does a trader know when it's too soon? Or too late?

Simply purchasing and holding an investment for many years can certainly work, but the investor must be willing to deal with volatile market conditions during that time.

Using the *buy and hold* strategy, a person's portfolio can easily go up ten percent within the first month, but then lose thirty percent of its value during the next five months.

Since the investor decided to hold, the portfolio is now down by twenty percent.

Over the next six months after that, the portfolio might increase by fifty percent, leaving the investor with a thirty percent gain in a year.

A thirty percent return in a year is good. But why not take the ten percent profit before the profits diminish, and then get back into the trade with more money when there is a good chance that the bottom is in?

Getting in and out at the right times can allow the investor to use more capital on the next trade.

To illustrate using the above example, let's say two different investors are using $100,000 each to buy the same stock.

The investor using the *buy and hold* strategy will go from $100,000 to $110,000 in the first month, after the ten percent increase in value. By the end of the sixth month, this investor's portfolio will be down to $77,000, after the thirty percent decline from $110,000. After the fifty percent increase, the portfolio will go from $77,000 to $115,500. Satisfied with the return, the investor decides to close the position.

Now let's take a look at what could happen if the other investor exits and reenters at the correct times.

This investor's portfolio will go from $100,000 to $110,00 in the first month. Seeing that it's a fairly good time to take profit, the investor closes the position entirely. After avoiding the twenty percent decline over the following five months, the investor reenters with $110,000, then watches the portfolio increase by fifty percent over the next six months. After closing the position entirely, the investor is now left with $165,000, before moving on to a different investment. Now this investor has $165,000 to put into the next investment, instead of $115,000.

Both investors in the example started with the same amount of capital. They also bought the same stock around the same time.

But at the end of the twelve month period, one investor was in the green by $49,500 more than the investor who was using the *buy and hold* strategy.

A trader applying the *buy and hold* strategy might be very disciplined and unemotional in the marketplace, yet still struggle to produce the kind of results that are being sought after.

Commission fees will need to be paid to the broker each time a trade is executed, and those can add up.

But unless the trader is executing many trades in short periods of time, the fees are generally not expensive enough to justify a portfolio going into the red by thousands of dollars.

Of course, a trader can not be expected to "catch the exact bottom" or "hit the exact top" with perfect accuracy.

But knowing when a trend change is likely taking place can certainly help the trader make better decisions in the financial markets.

How can we know when a trend change is likely taking place?

How can we know when a stock is overbought?

How can we know if it's oversold?

How can we identify where and what the supply and demand is?

Technical analysis.

The amount of information out there is vast, and it can be overwhelming at times to decide how much of it is relevant to your particular situation.

Whether you are a short-term trader or long-term investor, using and applying technical analysis is important because you need to know when to enter and exit a position, regardless of the time frame.

You can separate yourself from the crowd that simply buys a stock and hopes that it will go up. Technical analysis makes it easier for a trader or investor to have a plan, rather than just hold onto a security blindly.

This book will focus on the technical analysis information that is most important, as well as how to apply it to become more profitable in the financial markets.

It will cover:

- **How to understand the different types of candlesticks**

- **How to know the price range of a trading period**

- **How to use candlesticks to avoid losses**

- **How to know if the share price is likely to ascend or descend**

- **How to use a chart to see if a trend is likely to reverse**

- **How to identify buy and sell signals on a chart**

- **How to determine how far a share price may ascend or decline**

- **and more**

Technical Analysis vs Fundamental Analysis

There are some technical analysts who believe that fundamental analysis is useless for the most part. While they bring up some valid points in their arguments, it can be difficult to offer a definitive answer as to whether one form of analysis is better than the other.

Personally, I don't like to trade the financial markets without doing technical analysis, and I tend to emphasize it in my trading routine to a greater extent than fundamental analysis.

But let's review what both of them are.

Technical analysis: The identification of patterns and trends through the use of charts to determine which direction a stock is most likely to be heading. This can be done by utilizing *trend lines*, *moving averages*, and many other indicators to locate popular price points for buying and selling based on what the stock has done in the past. This type of analysis also relies heavily on price action and the measurement of volume of shares being traded.

Fundamental analysis: The evaluation of securities by measuring their intrinsic value. Fundamental analysts typically try to stay updated on the latest news releases about the security. This type of analysis relies heavily on earnings reports, company management, and the shape of the overall economic environment.

Fundamental analysis can tell you if it's a good idea to invest in a certain company in the long term, while technical analysis can help identify a good time to get in.

A good company with plenty of potential is still prone to setbacks along the way. Some of these setbacks can be severe, and technical analysis can help a trader avoid large losses.

It's not necessarily a good time to buy just because you are expecting good news to come out about a company. Sometimes the price action does not reflect a positive news story that gets released, particularly if the security has been on a long-term decline.

Technical analysis does not allow you to see the future, but if used correctly, it can help the trader determine if they are paying too much for a security (or selling it for too little) at a particular time.

Generally, many investors and traders tend to agree that fundamental analysis should be used to determine which securities should be invested in, while technical analysis should be used to determine when to buy and sell.

How to Understand the Different Types of Candlesticks

If you have not already decided on a charting platform to use, trading view is one of the most popular ones available.

After you reach the website, select the **Launch Chart** tab, which is located toward the center of the screen on the main page. By default, you will be directed to the AAPL (symbol for *Apple*) page.

To switch to a different stock, simply click the AAPL ticker toward the top-left corner of the screen. This will highlight it. From there, type in the stock symbol you are looking for, and then select it from the list that pops up.

Regardless of which stock ticker you decide to view, the trading view website should display a chart with candlesticks on it. The candlesticks that take up the bulk of the screen are the ones that are displaying the price action.

The bars below the price action candlesticks are there to display the volume of shares being traded.

Volume is certainly an important part of trading, but this chapter will focus on the price action candlesticks.

How to Know the Price Range of a Trading Period

When looking meticulously at a candlestick chart, you will probably notice that not all of the candles look the same.

Some of them might have long upper wicks, while others might have long lower wicks.

If a lower wick on a candlestick had reached a price point of $9.75, and the upper wick had reached a price point of $10.25, the trading range for that particular time period was $9.75 to $10.25.

By default, the *trading view* website will set the time frame to the *Daily* chart. To change the time frame, select the **D** symbol toward the top-left corner of the screen, then select the desired time frame from the drop-down list.

The time frames that will be most beneficial to you will largely depend on what kind of trader you'd like to be.

A day trader will open and close a position in the same day. A swing trader will "swing" a position overnight and will often hold onto it for several days or weeks. Someone holding onto a position for months at a time will generally be considered a long-term investor.

Day traders tend to look at the 5 minute and 1 minute charts the most often, while sometimes paying attention to the daily chart. Swing traders tend to primarily utilize the 4 hour, daily, and weekly charts. Long-term investors can benefit from looking at monthly charts and making decisions based on that time frame.

Determining which trading style is best is a matter of personal preference. Some people decide to stick with day trading because they find it very risky to leave a position open overnight. This could largely be due to the possibility of news coming out that could negatively affect their investments after the trading session. Many news outlets wait until after the markets close before announcing something that is likely to impact the price of stocks.

I have tried trading on different time frames and have found my profit/loss ratios to be approximately the same, so it has led me to believe that swing trading is not necessarily more profitable than day trading.

How to Know Where the Opening and Closing of a Time frame is

The color of the candle will tell you where the candlestick opened and closed.

If the candlestick is red, that means the opening of the time frame was at the top of the solid candle body.

Note: a solid candle body does not include a wick. A wick indicates that the price did not stay at that particular region for very long. For example, if you are looking at a daily chart and a candlestick has a wick that reaches $5, but the top of the solid candle body only reaches the four dollar mark by the end of the trading day, that means that the price might have been trading at five dollars for a few hours or less, and soon went back down and eventually closed at $4. In this case, the high of the candle was five dollars, but it didn't stay at that price for very long, so a wick was formed.

The closing of the time frame happens at the bottom of the solid candle body of a red candle.

On a green candlestick, it's the opposite. The opening of the time frame happens at the bottom of the solid candle body. The closing of the time frame happens at the top of the solid candle body.

Tip: Some traders prefer to use black and white candlestick charts instead of red and green. The intention of some of these traders is to make the chart appear more boring.

When it comes to trading, boredom can actually be more beneficial than excitement and fear. Looking at the colorful red and green candles can stir up emotions more easily than the blander black and white ones.

Staying unemotional can prevent the trader from making irrational decisions that end of leading to losses.

If you are in a position, and you getting extremely excited when you see a green candle and panicky when you see a red candle, you might benefit from switching to the black and white candlestick chart.

Candlestick Names and Definitions

For a reference, here is a list of some of the common candlesticks that you are likely to encounter on a stock chart:

DOJI: Looks like a plus sign, a cross, or an inverted cross. The wick will take up the majority of the candlestick, leaving almost no candle body at all.

DRAGONFLY DOJI: A type of candle in which the wick takes up the majority of the candlestick and rests at the very top. It looks like the letter T.

GRAVESTONE DOJI: This candlestick looks like an upside down letter T.

LONG BODY/LONG DAY: A long candlestick. The majority of the candle body is solid, but has a small wick on the top and bottom.

LONG SHADOW: These are similar to the DOJI candles, but have just a little bit more of a solid candle body.

MARUBOZU: A solid candle without any wicks.

SPINNING TOP: As the name implies, this candlestick looks like a spinning top. It has a small candle body toward the center of the wick.

How to Use Candlesticks to Avoid Losses

Memorizing the names of candlesticks is not as important as knowing what they represent. The last section covered the definitions of some of the most common types of candlesticks.

Now it's time to understand how they can help you make more informed decisions in the financial marketplace.

But first, you will need to understand the difference between the "bulls" and the "bears."

Bullish market- this is when share prices are rising. "Bull" investors are buying stocks, believing that the share prices will increase.

Buying a stock with the intention of selling it later for profit after the stock goes up is called, taking out a "long" position, or "going long."

If a setup on a stock chart looks like it's calling for the price to go up, it is often referred to as "bullish."

Bearish market- this is when share prices are falling. "Bear" investors are "shorting" the stocks by borrowing them and selling them, believing that the share prices will decrease.

If successful, they buy back the shares for a cheaper price after the stock falls.

DOJI

The solid body is extremely small, and the lower wick is just as long as the upper wick, which means the buyers and sellers seem to be equally indecisive. This makes the trade increasingly risky because it is too unclear as to which way the market is heading.

$$+$$

If the candlestick looks like a plus sign, it's a good idea to stay out of the trade until more clarification is obtained.

If the candlestick looks like an inverted cross, it means the sellers were quicker to sell than the buyers were to buy. It's more bearish than bullish.

If the candlestick looks like a cross, it means the buyers were quicker to buy than the sellers were to sell. It's more bullish than bearish.

DRAGONFLY DOJI

$$\top$$

Since the candle body is all the way on the top, this means that the buyers were very quick to buy, which could be a bullish sign.

GRAVESTONE DOJI

$$\bot$$

Since the candle body is all the way at the bottom, this means that the sellers were very quick to sell, which could be a bearish sign.

Long Shadow

Since these candlesticks are so similar to the DOJI candlesticks, the same concepts apply.

MARUBOZU

A red MARUBOZU candlestick on a daily chart will open at the high of the day and close at the low of the day, which indicates that the sellers were in full control throughout the entire trading day.

A green MARUBOZU candlestick on the daily chart will open at the low of the day and close at the high of the day, indicating that the buyers were in full control throughout the entire trading day.

Since wicks are essentially nonexistent in this type of candlestick, it means the price action was very definitive.

If this candle is red on the daily chart, but the weekly chart recently had a series of green candles over the past month, this could indicate a good time to buy a security, as long as the candle is large enough.

The idea here is to find a stock that has been doing well in the longer term, but pulling back in the short term, so the trader can purchase it at a lower price. If it works out, the market will continue its upward trend after the sellers have "exhausted themselves."

If a stock has been on a long-term downtrend, this idea will be counterproductive. Buying the dip works fairly well in bull markets, not bear markets.

If a stock that has been steadily trending upwards for a few months suddenly encounters a five percent pullback in one day, there is a fair chance that the worst of the selloff is over, and if you are a swing trader, it could be a good stock to buy and hold overnight.

As a day trader, a strong hourly chart with a large pullback on the five minute or fifteen minute time frame, could indicate a good time to buy.

Picture it this way:

It's easier to preserve strength as a marathon runner than it is for a sprinter who is running at full speed.

A sprinter *could* surprise the crowd by continuing to sprint for a while, but generally, running at full speed is not done for a long period of time.

A large red candlestick is similar to the sprinters exhausting themselves, and if the stock has generally been bullish long-term, there is a good chance that the buyers will soon step back in to buy the "discounted" stock.

Even if this type of candlestick is technically bearish, since it is red and it closed at the low of the day, it can still indicate that it is a good time to buy, since the sellers are likely getting exhausted by using up such a large portion of their "selling power" all at once.

However, if the pullback is very drastic, such as thirty percent or more, this could indicate the beginning of a trend reversal, and this type of strategy would be negated in that case.

Look for a candlestick that shows a healthy pullback of approximately four to seven percent.

Another thing to watch out for is the history of the stock's price movement. If it is on a long-term uptrend, but has a history of pulling back fifteen to twenty percent during its rallies, it might be better to wait for a larger pullback before buying the security.

Long Body/Long Day

The strategy for the this candlestick can be mirrored by the same strategy explained for the MARUBOZU candlestick, since they are both so similar.

Spinning Top

A spinning top candlestick indicates indecision in the market. The price action is much less definitive with this type of candlestick because it shows that the buyers and sellers couldn't seem to make up their minds as to whether a stock was overbought or oversold.

It is often best to avoid making a trade when this type of candlestick presents itself because it is like flipping a coin.

The small candle body at the center of the wick shows that the buyers were very quick to buy and the sellers were very quick to sell. This can make it difficult to gain clarity as to where the market is heading.

Candlestick Patterns

The last section went over individual candlesticks. Now it's time to cover some of the common candlestick patterns and how you can use them to make more informed decisions in the financial markets.

Blue sky breakout

Generally, it's a good idea to wait for consolidation before taking out a long position on a security that has been ascending on the price charts.

But sometimes it continues to move up for several days or more, causing the traders who are waiting for an entry on the sidelines to feel like they are missing out on the big move.

In a relentless bull market, sometimes a trader is left with little choice but to jump into a security without waiting for it to dip a little bit.

A regular breakout is when a stock breaks above a resistance level, but there are still more resistance levels up ahead. A blue sky breakout is when the stock breaks through the final resistance level, leaving no other resistance points up ahead.

A resistance level is a zone that a security commonly gets rejected at, indicating that supply has exceeded demand.

During a blue sky breakout, you might see a series of green candles consecutively after resistance has been broken.

The trouble with blue sky breakouts is that by the time the stock takes out the final resistance zone, it is usually already overextended, which could lead to a significant pullback.

If you decide to jump into a blue sky breakout, it's important to watch the trade closely, and not to hold onto it for longer than a few days.

One way of knowing if the security will continue to go up is by assessing how much follow through the stock has after it breaks resistance. If it breaks resistance, but only by a few cents, that's not very good follow through.

Cup and handle

As the name implies, the candlesticks on the chart will resemble a cup and handle. The cup will be on the left side of the handle and it will be in the shape of the letter "U," while the handle will have a slight downward trend.

As long as the bottom has a "U" shape, it is considered bullish, so it presents a buying opportunity. If the bottom has more of a "V" shape, it is best avoided, as per technical analysis indicates.

The candlesticks travel in a "U" formation. After making the "U" shaped recovery, they will start trending slightly downward again.

Picture a downward slope at the top-right corner of the "U." The buy signal is presented during the consolidation period of the slight downtrend after the "U" shaped recovery.

A realistic profit target can be assessed by measuring the distance between the bottom of the "U" and the top of the "U."

If the move from the bottom of the cup to the top was twenty percent, the profit target could be twenty percent, with a stop loss placed slightly below the handle formation.

One of the drawbacks to playing a *cup and handle* pattern is that it can be difficult to tell if the cup is truly presenting a "U" or if it is actually a "V." Sometimes a sharp, V-looking bottom actually plays out quite well.

Another drawback is that the cup sometimes forms without the handle.

Dark cloud cover

This candlestick pattern is made up of two candles; a red candlestick that opens above the previous green candle body, and then closes below the green candle body's center.

It shows that buyers had stepped in early within that particular time frame, but were soon overpowered by significant selling pressure.

Piercing line

A bullish formation with a two-day reversal pattern.

This happens when a candle is long and red, and then the next candle is green and opens at a new low before closing above the midpoint of the previous candle's body.

Rising three methods

This is where three short red candlesticks stand between two long green candlesticks.

It is a bullish sign because it shows that the selling has been minimal compared to the buying.

Falling three methods

This is where three short green candlesticks stand between two long red candlesticks. This is a bearish sign because it shows that the buying has been minimal compared to the selling.

Three black crows

A pattern that develops when three red candles are formed in a row, and all of them have relatively short wicks or no wicks at all.

They will open near the closing price of the previous candle, but as selling pressure decreases, they get pushed down further.

This is bearish, as it displays that the sellers have continued the downtrend for three candles in a row.

However, the size of the candlesticks should be taken into consideration.

If they are very small compared to the green candles before them, it could just indicate that the stock is taking a healthy pullback.

Zoom out and look at the longer time frames to gain more clarification.

How to Know if the Share Price is Likely to Ascend or Descend

Although candlestick patterns can help you identify trend changes, there is still the question of whether or not the trend change is real or just a fake out.

Sometimes a trader will spot what appears to be a good opportunity to buy when the price breaks through resistance and begins trending upward, only to have the share price take a turn in the opposite direction and head back down again.

This is why knowing the volume of shares being traded in a given time period can be useful.

On a trading chart, the volume bars will be displayed toward the bottom of the screen. If you are looking at a daily chart, the volume bars will represent the amount of shares being traded for each particular day. If you are on an hourly chart, the volume bars will represent the amount of shares being traded for each particular hour, and so forth.

If bullish traders are looking to open a long position during an uptrend, they often like to see the bull volume increasing on the chart, just to give them the likelihood that the price of the security will continue to move up.

When bullish traders are looking to open a long position during a downtrend, they often like to see the bear volume decreasing, just to give them the added possibility that the downtrend might be coming to an end.

Picture the volume indicator as a speed gauge on a car. The car might still be moving forward in the intended direction, but if it's speed is decreasing, it is more likely to come to a stop.

If you saw a vehicle driving toward you on the road, and it went from thirty miles an hour to twenty miles an hour to ten miles an hour, you would probably assume that the driver was planning to stop the car entirely.

In the opposite case, if you see and hear a vehicle accelerating from down the road when a traffic light turns yellow, you would probably assume that the driver is planning on going through the red light.

As there are signs to look out for as a driver and pedestrian, there are also signs that offer clues as to whether a share price is going to continue increasing or decreasing.

Increasing volume is like increasing momentum. When the momentum looks like its drying up, there is a likelihood that the move is getting ready to slow down or stop.

In most cases, volume is strongly correlated to the size of the move on the price chart. The higher the volume, the higher the move in price. When there is a higher amount of volume than usual, the share price will likely be more volatile than it usually is.

If you see low volume for days at a time, and then the security suddenly makes a move that is accompanied by a large spike in volume, it can be a good indicator that the move was for real and that the price action movement has a fair chance of picking up in the near future.

The same thing goes for day trading. If volume has been low for an hour of so, and then it suddenly picks up drastically on a fifteen minute chart, there is a good chance that the price action is on the verge of picking up.

If experienced bullish traders are waiting to buy a security on a pullback, but notice that the bear volume is increasing, they often see that as a sign to stay on the sidelines and wait patiently for a better time to get in.

Knowing where the volume spike takes place is another important thing to consider.

When a security has been trending in a certain direction for a while with increasing volume, and then it suddenly has a large spike, the trend might not be sustainable for much longer.

If a bullish volume spike occurs toward the top of an uptrend, it is often an indication that the trend is coming to an end. This is sometimes referred to as a "volume climax."

If a bearish volume spike occurs toward the bottom of a downtrend, it is often an indication that the trend is coming to an end.

How to Use a Chart to See if a Trend is Likely to Reverse

One of the good things about technical analysis is that you can identify supply and demand areas on the chart.

Supply and demand can also be referred to as support and resistance.

Support areas are known as places on the chart where buyers have a history of purchasing a security and moving the price up.

Resistance areas are known as places on the chart where sellers have a history of unloading a security and driving the price back down.

Certain support and resistance areas are stronger than others, so it's important to pay attention to the strength level of each one that is nearby.

Essentially, the more often a price gets rejected at a certain price level, the stronger the resistance or support area becomes.

If a candlestick for a security that has been trading at an all-time high reaches the $20 mark on the daily chart, goes back down to $19.50 the next day, and then goes up to the $21 range a day or two after that, the $20 mark did not prove to be a very strong resistance area.

If the candlestick gets rejected at the $20 mark many times, it can be considered a strong resistance area because sellers were usually quick to take profits when it reached that area.

Simply looking for bases of support and ceilings of resistance on a chart can help determine the supply and demand levels for securities.

One way to go about it is to count the number of times a security has touched a certain price point on a chart before it moved in the opposite direction.

But another way to identify supply and demand areas is through the use of moving averages (MA).

Since moving averages can act as support and resistance gauges, they are popular tools for traders and investors.

There are two different types of moving averages; simple moving averages (SMA) and exponential moving averages (EMA).

Although both of these tools are used to measure the movement of securities, they are slightly different.

The main difference is that the exponential moving average directs its focus toward current price action, which makes it quicker to react to price movement.

The simple moving average distributes its focus more evenly towards past price movement and current price movement.

To illustrate how a simple moving average works, here is a series of prices over a five trading day period SMA(5):

$5

$6

$7

$8

$9

Simple moving average calculation:

5+6+7+8+9 = 35

Five day period simple moving average:

35/5 = 7

The SMA for the five day trading period is $7.

When the price of a security is trading above a moving average, that moving average is considered a support area.

When the share price is trading below the moving average, the moving average is considered resistance.

Generally, the longer the time frame is, the stronger the moving average becomes, so a 200 day moving average would usually be stronger than a 10 day moving average.

To gain balance, you can use multiple moving average time frames on a chart.

For example, a trader might want to use a 10 day EMA, 100 day EMA, and a 200 EMA all on the same screen to get a bigger picture of what is happening.

If you are a long-term investor, you can use weekly moving averages or monthly moving averages on the chart.

To bring up the Exponential moving average on trading view:

1.) Select the **Indicators & Strategies** tab on the top of the screen.

2.) Type EMA into the search box and press the **Enter** key on your keyboard.

3.) The EMA symbol should now be posted near the top-left corner of the screen. Close the **Indicators & Strategies** window.

4.) Next to the EMA symbol, select the *Settings* tab.

5.) Under the **Length** section, adjust the parameter to the number you'd like to use. If you are using the daily chart, selecting the number "10" will display the 10-day exponential moving average.

6.) After setting the parameter to the number you'd like to use, select the **OK** tab.

If a security holds a certain support level for a long time, and then breaks it, that major support level can often act as a major resistance later on.

In bear markets, old support tends to become new resistance. In bull markets, old resistance often act as new support.

On the candlestick chart, the solid candle body will need to close below the support line in order to confirm that it has been broken.

If it simply "wicks" down past the support line, that doesn't necessarily count as breaking support because the buyers were very quick to buy. The close of the solid body of the candlestick is what matters significantly in this case.

Once the support has been broken, another thing to pay attention to is volume. If support is broken, but the volume is very low, the move might not end up having much follow through afterward.

How to Identify Buy and Sell Signals on a Chart

In addition to volume and moving averages, there is another common tool that many traders use to tell if it is a good time to buy or sell a security.

When a stock is overbought, that is often a sign that a trader should sell it. When a stock is oversold, that can often be a good opportunity for a trader to buy it.

You can find out if a stock is overbought or oversold by looking at the Relative Strength Index (RSI) indicator.

The numbers on the scale of the Relative Strength Index go from 0 to 100. On this scale, the number "30" indicates that the stock is oversold, while the number "70" indicates that it's overbought.

When the RSI on the weekly chart is oversold, that usually means that the stock has been in a long-term downtrend.

But if the RSI is oversold on the 1 hour chart, this could be a good time to buy if the longer-term trend has been upward.

When a stock has a strong daily chart, but an oversold hourly chart, that could be a sign that it is forming a higher low on the daily chart.

As long as the stock is forming higher lows and higher highs on the longer-term time frames, it is considered bullish. But it's usually not a good idea to buy a stock when it's forming a higher high. It is often better to wait for a pullback, or in this case, a higher low.

To get the most out of the RSI indicator, it helps to review the stock's history of RSI levels. If the stock has a history of staying in oversold region for days or weeks at a time, it's probably not going to be a good idea to buy it as soon as it gets oversold,s since it hasn't been respecting the RSI territories.

But if a stock has been respecting the RSI territories by bouncing off of them, the trader should be able to make a more accurate decision based on the Relative Strength Index.

In a bear market, a stock might trade between the 25 to 40 level on the RSI indicator's weekly chart for weeks at a time.

In a bull market, it's not uncommon for a stock to trade between the 50 to 85 level for weeks at a time.

That's one of the reasons why it's important to know what kind of market you are dealing with. If it's a very strong bull market, and you are waiting for the RSI to pull back to oversold on the daily chart before you buy shares, you might have to wait for a long time.

If the stock has been very bearish on the daily chart, it won't make much sense to buy shares as soon as the RSI reaches oversold, since it can stay oversold for a while.

When different time frames start aligning with each other, it will improve the odds of a successful trade.

For example, if the 4 hour, daily, and weekly RSI are all oversold in a bear market, it could improve the trader's chances of making a successful trade if he or she decides to buy.

But even then, the trader will be trading against the trend, so it's usually better to be quick to take profit in such a case.

How to Determine How Far a Share Price May Ascend or Decline

An earlier chapter already covered how to know if a share price is likely to ascend or descend, but this chapter will cover how far it is likely to go.

Since moving averages can act as support and resistance, they will give a fairly good idea of how far a share price might go before it changes direction.

But another way of determining support and resistance areas is through the use of trend lines.

The idea is to draw one or more trend lines on the chart, usually one to represent support and another to represent resistance.

The resistance line can be drawn from the top high of a recent trend to the bottom high. For example, if a recent rally reached a high of $100 per share and descended to a recent lower high of $50 per share, the trend line can be drawn from the top of the $100 candlestick to the top of the $50 candlestick.

The support line can be drawn from top low of the recent trend to the bottom low. If the highest low of the recent rally reached $95 per share and descended to a recent lower low of $45, the trend line can be drawn from the bottom of the $95 candlestick to the bottom of the $45 candlestick.

Some traders prefer to ignore the wicks in this case and focus on the solid candle body, so the trend lines would be drawn from the tops and bottoms of the solid candle bodies.

When drawing a resistance trend line, it's important to make sure that none of candle tops are closing below or too far above it, as this would render the trend line invalid. Try to keep the price points aligned with the trend line.

The same thing goes for the support line. Try to make sure that none of the candle bottoms close below the trend line or too high above it.

The idea is to draw them further than where the current price is, so you can see where the price range might be heading if the trend continues.

After the trend lines have been drawn, it can give the trader an estimated price range of where the stock may bounce back and forth in.

For example, if the trend lines have been drawn from the candlesticks that are dating from five weeks ago to the current date, following the pattern of the trend line, continue to extend it to a later date.

If the stock has been trading between $45 per share and $95 per share over the past five weeks, a trader can extend the trend lines two weeks into the future on the chart to see what it might be trading at if the trend were to continue.

After the lines are drawn out a couple of weeks into the future on the chart, the trader might find the support and resistance zones to be at $25 for support and $35 for resistance.

This can be used as one way of knowing what the resistance and support lines will likely be in the upcoming days.

The trend lines remain valid as long as the stock's share price trades within that channel.

Of course, since this is like trying to forecast the future, these trend lines can break sooner than a trader might anticipate. They should only be used to gain a general idea of where the stock might be trading if the pattern continues.

    To use the trend line feature in trading view, select the Trend Line tab on the left side of the screen.

Closing

Remaining profitable in the financial markets can be very challenging, especially as a beginner. But gaining experience and utilizing technical analysis correctly can improve a trader's odds of obtaining long-term success.

But you need to have a strategy and stick to it. Whether your strategy is to buy an oversold bounce and sell when the RSI reaches overbought levels, or to simply dollar cost average and hold long-term, it's important not to let emotions gain control.

A good way to take emotion out of the trade is to not look at it as making or losing money. Try to think of it as just numbers on a screen.

If many trades are being lost in a short period of time, it is usually better to simply stop trading for a while. Emphasize education, then start trading again, but with smaller share sizes the next time around.

Technical analysis is not magic, so it's unrealistic to expect it to play out as anticipated every single time.

As the market changes, your strategies might also need to change in order to stay profitable.

Staying disciplined and focused while trading or investing is critical.

www.ingramcontent.com/pod-product-compliance
Lightning Source LLC
Chambersburg PA
CBHW030017190526
45157CB00016B/3108